LET
US
TALK

LET US TALK

Dwarka Ramphal, Ph.D.

Kravitz & Sons

Kravitz and Sons LLC
1301 Farmville Blvd, Suite 104
Greenville, NC 27834

© 2024 Dwarka Ramphal, Ph.D. All rights reserved.

No part of this book may be reproduced, stored in a retrieval system, ortransmitted by any means without the written permission of the author.

Published by Kravitz and Sons LLC.

ISBN: 979-8-89639-040-4 (sc)
ISBN: 979-8-89639-039-8 (e)

Library of Congress Control Number: 2024925107

Because of the dynamic nature of the Internet, any web addresses or linkscontained in this book may have changed since publication and may no longer bevalid. The views expressed in this work are solely those of the author and do notnecessarily reflect the views of the publisher, and the publisher hereby disclaims any responsibility for them.

Contents

Acknowledgements

I most gratefully express my sincerest thanks to the following persons without whom this publication could not have been a reality:

Mrs. Patricia Dickenson and Mrs. Malvern Williams, who devoted and sacrificed much time in typing the manuscript;

Miss Gia Knowles and Mrs. Julie Glover, who assisted with research and material;

The students, staff, administration, and board of Saint Paul's College and all my friends; My brothers and sisters and my wife, Rita, and my children,

Rudra and Zhenya, who have sacrificed so much to make this possible;

Those not mentioned who made a tremendous contribution to this publication.

Heartiest thanks.

I also wish to acknowledge contributions from the following persons and companies:

Greg Smith,
Julie Glover,
Kennard Ramphal,
Chaitram Ramphal,
Chandra Turner, and
Shell Bahamas (Freeport).

Introduction

On investigating English language teaching/English language learning in the Bahama Islands, I became aware of a much greater problem which exists universally. This problem has to do, not only with our approach to educational establishments, but also with the superimposition of cultures and nations through these establishments. This linguistic colonialism is the basis on which our educational institutions are built.

The fact that we all went to school to learn English has left us with a belief that schooling is the only source of true education and certification is the ultimate measurement of performance.

It was a very shattering experience when I began to question these long-standing assumptions, but I dare say that this shattering has proven most liberating. When one begins to question the status quo, one is branded radical and revolutionary. I make no claim for myself. I only claim the right to question and to seek answers so that ultimately we can create for ourselves and generations to come a peaceful and mutually intelligible and respectable world.

The references I have made to Grand Bahama are mere illustrations of the world at large.

I encourage everyone who reads this book not to indulge in the dialogue of the deaf, but choose the road to the living word—and live.

One

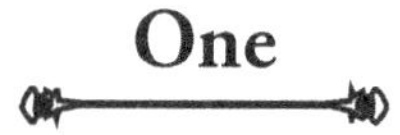

What Is Standard English?

Ever learning and never able to come to the knowledge of the truth.
—2 Timothy 3:5

This chapter discusses the concept of standardization in the Bahamas as a dialect-speaking community. The implications, however, are universal.

Assuming that there ought to be a language arts programme in the Bahamas, assuming that this language arts programme in the Bahamas has a sound philosophy underlying it, assuming that the teachers have the appropriate socio-psycho-linguistic orientation so that learning can take place, we still would be faced with that profound dilemma—what is to be taught?

To the unwary, this is a nonquestion. To the alert administrator, the evasive answer is "Teach standard English." It is this ethereal standard that eludes us all the time. Is standard English a language that is spoken by someone, somewhere, and at sometime? If that is the case, then the student should be taken to that person, at that place, at that time, to learn all the psychological and sociological aura associated with the standard language phenomenon.

I want, at the very outset, to postulate the following:

1. That the pursuit of standard is the chasing of a mirage.
2. That if that standard does exist, it exists as a dead language.
3. That the forced use of any dead language inhibits the normal development (especially the intuitive nature) of any human being.

Helen and Carl Lefevre asked the question, "What is correct [or standard] English?" To this question they answered, "There is no single correct English but a variety of English styles, patterns, and usages to match the needs of various speakers and writers and the widely varied situations in which they speak and write."[1]

Wherever you go in the English-speaking world, you will find a standard national or regional version of English speech. Lefevre embraced the notion that standard English can be defined as the language in which the main business of any English speech community is carried on.

George Cave (University of Guyana) described standard Guyanese English as the language spoken by the educated urban middle class on formal occasions.

Lefevre's definition embraces more than half of the society's language continuum. Furthermore, it depends on who is conducting the business and what is the "main business." This may be deliberate since Lefevre has already established that "There is no single correct English." Cave's problems begin when we try to find this educated urban middle-class person and ask him to speak on a formal occasion. He then has his own ideolect to contend with as a starter. As we record his speech, we realize that it fluctuates in standardization within itself, and is markedly different from another person of the same social class on the same occasion. The wheel has gone full circle. We are back where we started—what is standard?

The tragedy, however, is not only that "correct English" does not exist. The tragedy is that the teacher endows himself/herself with omniscience and teaches what he/she perceives to be "correct English." The examiner thinks that he knows better, and in spite of what the teacher has taught, fails the students (see appendix 1 for examinations written). Students, teachers, and examiner vigorously pursue the standard. Alas, it was only a mirage—we all end up in the same desert.

The problem is further complicated when we resolve our language problems by resorting to the lexical jungle-the dictionary. The dictionary has its place in society, but it was not meant to be abused in proclaiming the standard—every new edition of the dictionary is better than the previous one and every new edition is outdated before it is published. In fact, the compilers of the *New English Dictionary* "did not pretend to lay down a certain 'correct' way of using a word, but showed us the various uses to which it had been put at various times in the past. They bring home to us the idea of language as a living, growing thing, not as something that can ever be fixed."[2]

Language is not static. In fact it is not only dynamic, it is volatile. By the time the textbooks have tried to standardize English, the language has moved hours away. The only standard we are left with is the heritage of the textbooks, and even as we read it, this "standard language" has been dead a long time ago.

One of the most significant farces that has existed for many years is when the teacher forces the student to use "standard English" or "correct English." Every year it becomes clearer that the student cannot produce this "standard." The student is regarded as "stupid" and "lazy" and his creativity is murdered and buried. At the end of his school career, the teacher proudly awards him an R.I.P. (Rest In Peace) for creativity. We have succeeded, through language teaching, in destroying another person.

Notes

1. Helen and Cari Lefevre, Writing by Patterns (New York: Alfred A. Knopf, 1978).
2. David Brazil, The True Book about Our Language (London: Frederich Ltd., 1965) 96.

Two

Which Standard to Teach?

Newspeak was the official language of Oceania and has been devised to meet the ideological needs of Ingsoc, or English socialism. The purpose of Newspeak was … to make all other modes of thought impossible.

—George Orwell
Nineteen Eighty-Four

Even if, perchance, we can arrive at a definition for "standard" English in a specific community, we still have the problem in the Bahamas and the Caribbean—which standard to teach?

The problem of what to teach in the Bahamas is more serious than driving left-hand-drive cars on the left hand side of the road. The situation here is that 90 percent of the cars are American, but the traffic laws are British.

Historically, the Bahamas was a British colony for more than three hundred years. Like the rest of the English-speaking Caribbean, it has developed out of colonization and, as is inevitable, has adapted the dispositions of the mother country. Its target, supposedly, was to speak like the Englishman and even today some Bahamians pride themselves in being able to speak like the British.

Politically, the governor general of the Bahamas is still a representative of the crown. The Commonwealth of the Bahamas is still a member of the British Commonwealth. Many of the institutions were established by Englishmen who brought with them their language and culture.

It is not surprising, therefore, that there should be such a great "British English" influence in the Bahamas. Many teachers use this as a cue to decide that we must teach "the King's English" (or is it "the

Queen's English")? This concept is reinforced in that representatives from the ministry of education go once every year to Great Britain to recruit teachers for the Bahamas. We must note that this is a political decision and not a linguistic one, albeit it still reflects a tendency towards standardization according to British norm. Even educators can be deceived into thinking that the British English standard is the measuring rod by which English is measured around the world.

Contrary to the aspirations of pseudoeducators, the populace in many cases is exposed to English, American style. This time it is economics that determines language. Thousands of tourists from the United States come to the Bahamas every year and provide the main source of income for the country. These tourists interact with people from all levels of society—from the boy selling conch shells in the marketplace to the manager of the hotel—and rub off their linguistic jargon on a large section of the community. This, however, is not the only influence of American English.

The greatest influence of American English comes through television. In Grand Bahama, the seven television channels available are all from Florida. Needless to say, students spend a great deal of their time looking at television and much of the knowledge acquired is through the television. Many teachers combine economics and television media to conclude that the best thing to teach in the Bahamas is "standard" American English.

Geographically, however, the Bahamas shares the common waters of the West Indies. The cultural and linguistic heritage is one with the Caribbean people, and as Dennis Craig puts it in a discussion with teachers in Grand Bahama, "the Caribbean is one region . . . and we must destroy the assumption that English is the mother tongue of our students." The Bahamas conforms to a common West Indian dialect which developed out of the same type of colonialism. The lexis (resulting from the native food and culture) are largely similar and the syntax is to a great extent, West African, just like the other Creoles of the English-speaking Caribbean.

By virtue of proximity, history, and culture, the Bahamas can associate with some form of West Indian English.

Then comes Shilling and Holm, who concede that there is a "standard Bahamian English" but describe it in relation to Caribbean

Creoles. They noted that "Bahamian English forms a link between the Caribbean Creoles such as Jamaican English, and the English spoken today by many black people in the United States . . . Like most other Creole languages, Bahamian English arose from a collision of languages and cultures under the social conditions of slavery . . . One important result of this simplification was a loss of inflexional endings . . . "[1]

Notice carefully the use of the word *simplification*, not enrichment. The fact that you have drawn from several linguistic cultures does not matter at this time. What matters is that there are no inflexional endings. If we use this argument, would it not be reasonable to assume that English is a simplistic language, because we do not add plural markers to our adjectives, and Spanish and the French do?

Albeit there exists, however, a Bahamian English which varies in all the Islands of the Commonwealth, and yet remains peculiar to the Bahamas. Is it this unwritten, undescribed language one is expected to teach in the classrooms?

As the situation exists at present, the same language arts teacher teaches Bahamian English for the Bahamas Junior Certificate in grade nine, British English for the General Certificate of Education examination in grades ten and eleven, American English for the Scholastic Aptitude Test in grade twelve, and West Indian English, if the student is to identify with the literary tradition.

In this linguistic melting pot, the child's *langue* (or competence) is almost always ignored in the classroom and relegated to the realm of nonlanguage.

NOTES

1. Alison Shilling and John Holm, *Dictionary of Bahamian English* (New York: Lexik House Publications, 1982), iii.

Three

Is Nonstandard Dialect Incorrect?

Speak the speech I pray you, as I pronounced it to you.
—Shakespeare

Like the other Islands of the Caribbean, the people of the Bahamas speak a dialect of their own. Within the Bahamas this dialect varies from island to island, and there is enough socioeconomic stratification of the dialect to describe it in terms of acrolect, moselect, and basilect. Like the other Caribbean dialects, Bahamian dialect draws much of its lexis from English, and its structure from West African languages.

Albeit, this has not been described by linguists (even though Shilling and Holm attempted A *Dictionary of Bahamian English*) and because of this, many persons have not yet recognised the existence of the dialect. To ignore the Bahamian Creole is to fall prey to the false security of the ostrich; to attempt to wipe it out by stringent school rules and regulations is to be guilty of linguistic genocide.

This nonacceptance of Bahamian dialect is not peculiar to the classroom. Political authorities lend little credence to this language and opt instead for erasing from society this "bad English." Social groups of "middle class" Bahamians mock the speakers of dialect, and view them as ignorant, unschooled, and decadent. Students at school would not like to be regarded as speakers or writers of Bahamian dialect, because that would mean that they would be relegated to the lower echelons of society.

One can maybe understand, if not tolerate, the superimposition of a foreign English dialect by foreigners on a Bahamian community of dialect speakers. What is tragic, however, are the implications and attitude associated with such an imposition—the feeling that Bahamian dialect is a nonlanguage, a "bad English," adopted by the "dumb" and the "ignorant."

Of course, linguists themselves form part of the system, and in spite of their quest to ascertain the rightful place of national or regional dialects, they are still many times bound in shallows of miseries and doubts. One of the great linguistic fallacies of this century is the classification of dialects into acrolect, mesolect, and basilect, and the way it is represented in diagram (see appendix 2).

The shorter *Oxford Dictionary* (1947) states that the stem *acro* means terminal, topmost, a tip, peak, summit, the stem *meso* means middle, and the stem *basi* means pertaining to, situated at, or forming the base of. The implications of these terms are obvious and are contradictory to the claim of linguistics that does not support the superiority of any language.

If conscientious linguists are using these terms and representing them in such a way as to suggest that the basilect is a "base" language, then the prescriptive grammarians certainly have a case.

The inference of the terms *acrolect* and *basilect* are phenomenologically gross. If we are describing dialects, why not say that the form which is furthest removed from the standard is the highest form? This is not a mere quibble over semantics, but a conditioning of our minds by the use of words to foster a monstrous display of education for domestication and the fostering of a superior social class structure.

Shilling and Holm constantly refer to "the result of this simplification" and "these simplified languages" in discussing Bahamian dialect.[1]

Dell Hymes posits about dialects:

Because of their origins, however, their association with poorer and darker members of the society, and through perpetuation of misleading stereotypes—such as that a pidgin is merely a broken or baby talk version of another language—much interest, even where positive, has considered them merely curiosities. Much of the interest and information, scholarly as well as public, has been prejudicial. The languages have been considered, not creative adaptations, but degenerations; not systems in their own right, but deviations from other systems. Their origins have been explained, not by historical and social forces, but by inherent ignorance, indolence, and inferiority. Not the least of the crimes of colonialism has been to persuade the colonized that they, or ways in which they differ, are inferior to convince the stigmatized that the stigma is deserved.[2]

As discussed elsewhere, the truth is that language and culture are inseparable and it is the culture of basilect speakers that is rejected.

For effective teaching to take place, it is imperative that certain assumptions be destroyed. One such assumption is that English is the mother tongue of students in the Bahamas. The second is that the Bahamian dialect is "bad English."

Not to destroy these assumptions is to allow the students to innocently proceed to the maze of confusion and hypercorrection. In aspiring to obtain linguistic acceptance, the student attempts to imitate alien models and culminates in producing unfamiliar items. For example, "I is going," rather than (a going), or phonologically [ider] instead of [idye]. Marking what the student perceives as correct to be incorrect adds to the confusion of the student and inhibits linguistic creativity. Hypercorrection, undercorrection, and dialect usage are, to the unwary teachers, sources of extreme frustration and this frustration is transferred to the whole classroom in dealing with the dialect problem. The teacher invariably commits linguistic genocide, and the general effect is that the child does not learn.

NOTES

1. Alison Shilling and John Holm, *Dictionary of Bahamian English* (New York: Lexington House Publications, 1982), i, iv.
2. Dell Hymes, *Pidginization and Creolization of Language* (London: Cambridge University Press, 1971), preface.

Four

The Teacher without Philosophy

If I am to teach always, how am I to learn?
                                    — Galileo

Fixedness in language teaching contradicts the very definition of language in terms of its dynamic and creative nature. Kennard Ramphal in his dissertation opined that "The behaviour of teachers working with these students (nonstandard dialect speakers) is assumed to reflect the beliefs about the language and culture."[1] What the teacher believes about the language and culture of the student determines his or her reaction to the student (self-fulfilling prophecy will be discussed in chapter six). As aforementioned, teachers tend to relegate nonstandard dialect speakers to the realms of illiteracy and ignorance and the child responds by submerging himself in the culture of silence.

Even to suggest that there should be a language-teaching programme in a school is to fall prey to the following presuppositions:

1. The child has grown up learning the incorrect language.
2. That the teacher must superimpose the correct language on the child.
3. That the teacher is the one who knows the correct language and what constitutes correct language.
4.   That the language spoken by everyone in the society in which the child grows up is wrong.

All these fallacies culminate in the nonphilosophy of language teaching and covertly demonstrate a non liberation process of language usage. The philosophy of institutionalization and ritualization lends itself to Illich's process of domestication.

The teacher who does not take cognizance of the language acquired by the child and the language used everyday by the child has failed from the beginning. It is in the language of the child that thoughts are formed and complex processes are worked out. To shatter the everyday language of the child is to shatter the child's personality, which becomes irredeemable in the entire life of the individual.

By contrast, to enhance and support the language of the child is to offer the opportunity for a positive self-image. The child is then able to decipher intricate problems and be more analytic and evaluative.

If a teacher tries to superimpose a so-called standard dialect, the teacher may be inferring that one language is superior to the next. Even social differences in language must not innately deceive us to believe that one language is superior to the other.

As a further development, if we educators are the ones to determine the "rights" of language, then we are aligning ourselves with the bourgeoisie and oppression, and defeating the very purpose of education for liberation. Moreover, we are completely ignoring the creative and ever-changing nature of language and are ever grappling with irrelevant, archaic forms of language which resembles Latin in the way of the school boy's elegy:

Latin [or English in this case] is a dead language
As dead as can be
It killed the ancient Romans
And now it is killing me.

The dynamics of language are such that the pursuit for puritanism in language is the chasing of a mirage and can end only in despair and frustration. The frustration is then taken out on the student who is robbed of his sense of humour and so cannot laugh at the humour of language, but must rather bear his burden meekly and become doubly frustrated.

Where can we draw the line between accepted and unaccepted social standards? It is this question that leads us to our doom, The fact is that we cannot and must not attempt it. It is society which must determine what it wants to accept as standard, what it would reject, or what it would retain for peripheral reference. Too often we regard language as a blueprint for an engineering project, or we try to make decisions that we are totally incapable of making. It is more important that we *learn* language than *teach* language. When we stop learning language, we might as well concede that we have ceased to exist. *Cogito ergo sum*— I think, therefore, I exist. Language is directly related to the thought, so when, I use language I know that I am thinking and existing.

The language teaching philosophy needs to be far more than "I am, you are, he/she/or it is." It must embrace the very concept of individuality, personal freedom, societal freedom, and national freedom. The " . . . institutionalization of language (by schooling) confuses the teaching with learning, grade advancement with education, a diploma with competence and fluency with the ability to say something new. This leads inevitably to physical pollution, social polarization, and psychological incompetence; three dimensions in a process of global degradation and modernized misery."[2] Those who use dialect are certified for the treatment of their alleged disproportionate deficiencies.

Maybe domestication is understandable because it assigns to the teacher absolute knowledge and authority which always lends itself to abuse. The teacher becomes the oppressor, the student becomes the oppressed, and the dehumanization chain reaction is set off. The oppressors". . . who oppress and exploit by virtue of their power cannot find in this power the strength to liberate either the oppressed or themselves."[3] The oppressed do not seek liberation because as soon as they are old enough they can identify with the oppressive class, or even if they do not become teachers they can lay claim to social polarization at the upper end.

NOTES

1. Kennard Ramphal, "An Anlaysis of Reading Instructio Offered to West Indian Creole-speaking Students" (Ph.D. diss., University of Toronto, 1983), 8.

2. Ivan Illich, *Deschooling Society* (New York: Harper and Row, 1983), 1. Copyright 1970, 1971 by Ivan Illich. This and all following excerpts from *Deschooling Society* are reprinted by permission of Harper & Row, Publishers, Inc.

3. Paulo Freire, *Pedagogy of the Oppressed* (New York: Seabury Press, 1969), 28.

Five

The Socio-psycho-linguistic Factor

The linguistic preparation of prospective English teachers is woefully inadequate.

—Roger Shuy

The sociological factors affecting language teaching in the Bahamas are many and varied. But the society itself is so enslaved in foreign standards that it becomes afraid of its own freedom. As a result, it rejects its cultural heritage which is undeniably inherent in its linguistic identity.

In discussing the way language shapes concept and culture, Robert Ponge puts it this way:

> One function of language is communication within the society it belongs to. Since language cannot exist without context, and context is not only situational but also cultural, it follows that language is inseparable from the culture it gives a linguistic form to. When you express yourself fluently in a foreign language you do not translate, you start from concepts and put them across in language. If you cannot do so, it is because of the cultural gap: you are manipulating concepts springing from your (foreign) nature language. In order to effect communication, you have to re-shape your concepts so they can be expressed in the target language and can be understood by the other cultured receiver.
>
> Linguistically and educationally, if you separate a language from the culture, it is part of, you implicitly deny the existence of that culture. If you use that language, artificially divorced from its cultural matrix to express your own culture, you are

enslaving that language and its inseparable culture to your own needs, granting its existence only because of your own existence and worth, and not independently from yourself, and your values: it is by implication, if not explicitly, an exercise in cultural annexation.[1]

Paul Keens Douglas from Trinidad purports:

We are dialect people and yet we very seldom use dialect headlines. When we talk about attracting people to come to church, we don't use dialect headlines, we run the traditional statements, but you are not talking to people, you are talking to dialect people. Our radio and television are mainly to broadcast to our people so it should be in the kind of terms that our people can understand, but we put it in terms as if we are broadcasting to the rest of the world.

Let the rest of the world make the effort to understand us. If they are really interested they will very well come down and understand what we are saying. But instead of that we change everything we have so that they can understand, and we confuse our own people. So, people are walking around here confused because they don't understand what is being said, and confusion is a very big problem in language.[2]

In the social context, the language arts teacher must also be pitied. He/she is a kind of archetypal Sisyphus who needs to roll the stone to the top of the hill, thereby achieving the notion of correctness. Every time however, he/she is certain that the goal is at last attainable, society synthesizes novel structures and rules, and the teacher finds that he/she needs to adapt his concept of correctness, and the stone comes rolling down again. It is a pitiable sight to see the teacher start all over again.

The quest for linguistic perfection can only result in societal ostracism equivalent to the fate of Tantalus. The teacher suffer eternal hunger and thirst, never being able to conceive the attainment of perfection, because like Tantalus, he stands in a river of receding waters, overshadowed by the fruit trees with receding branches. Society determines standard language, but never defines it.

This is where prescriptive linguists and prescriptive grammarians become dangerously dogmatic. It is the descriptive linguist who holds the key to salvation, because he describes irrespective of cultural or societal biases.

Psychologically, the language teaching programme in high school has little foundation. Noam Chomsky, in discussing learning problems, introduces the concept of the Language Acquisition Device (L.A.D.). He further observed that "The tremendous intellectual accomplishment of language acquisition is carried out at a period of life when the child is capable of little else and that this task is entirely beyond the capabilities of an otherwise intelligent ape . . . even to speak of familiar sentences is an absurdity."[3]

By the age of five, the child has totally internalized all the rules that govern his own linguistic society. In fact, in the next fifty or sixty years of his life we can never teach him the equivalent of what he has acquired in those formative years, neither can we unteach him what he has learned in those years.

The rigors of the classroom negate the creativity and innate nature of language. This attitude regards language acquisition as less complex than a calculator and language use becomes a matter of learning and drills. It is this simplistic approach that creates mechanical language users who lack intuition and imagination.

The idea that sentences can be learned by conditioning or training, as proposed by the behaviorists, contradicts the obvious and rejects a commonsense approach. Language is not a matter of rote learning and habit. The child master's the semantic, syntactic, and phonological rules unconsciously and discretely, distinguishing the difference between deep structure and surface structure even though apparently similar, e.g., (a) Someone expected the doctor to examine John, (b) Someone persuaded the doctor to examine John.

It is up to the individual to discover and rediscover language and to reshape language like the healer's hand.

Even in the teaching of foreign languages we have found it more useful to use a total immersion method by which the student is surrounded by users of the foreign language. He/she learns quickly in that situation. Needless to say, that the learner appreciates fully the contextual use of the object language. Yet in our current English teaching programmes, we isolate the target language of the classroom from the language of the society.

LANGUAGE USAGE

The priority in language acquisition is to be language specific. The user must be able to say exactly what he wants to say and in a way that can be understood by the listener. He must develop:

1. Clarity
2. Specificity
3. An ability to use the mutual code
4. Creativity

Second, in language teaching the goal is to have the student understand readily what is being communicated to him or her. This entails:

1. Listening skills
2. A thorough knowledge of the code used both at the superficial level and the connotative level
3. Judging tone, emotion, and abstract values associated with the message since writing is just a poor attempt to reduce speech to the visual, the writing techniques are merely mechanical and generally reflect what the person can produce vocally.

The same can be said of aural comprehension and writing comprehension, where reading and understanding are secondary to listening and understanding. We are just repeating the accepted view that listening and speaking are basic to language acquisition at any level. In fact, it would seem as if Chomsky's L.A.D. becomes activated more readily by the facets which are basic to language.

CLARITY

The abuse of language is so great that it has given birth to the cliché that only a fool speaks when he has nothing to say but only a wise man speaks by saying nothing. Lewis Carroll has most profoundly shown us that words can be created, and existing words can be used creatively.

He also shows us that word usage can take ridiculous proportions and convey a spectrum of meanings.

SPECIFICITY

Every language user uses the lexicographer's technique to distinguish one item from every other item. The referential meaning must be exact and accurate. If there is confusion at the surface level, then it is useless to discuss deep structure to the extent that language needs to be specific. Even then, however, definitiveness in language can never be absolute and even words are never exactly specific.

CREATIVITY

Each language, each dialect of the language of even the most unsophisticated culture, can be creative enough to say what the speaker intends to communicate. The limits of expression of any language are infinite, and so on this basis, all languages are equal.

In teaching language, therefore, it will be more beneficial for the teacher to deal with language usage and the process of communication as a whole rather than isolated issues of a preconceived notion of correctness.

NOTES

1. Robert Ponge, "Foreign Language Teaching and the Two Cultures," Savocou, September 1975.
2. Paul Keens Douglas, "Communication and the Arts," Caribbean Contact, October 1984, 11. Used by permission.
3. Noam Chomsky, Recent Contributions to the Theory of Innate Ideas: Children with Learning Problems, ed. Edward Sapir et al. (New York: Brunner/ Mazel, 1973), 101.

Six

The Abuse of Language Teaching

To teach or not to teach, that is the question.

THE SELF-FULFILLING PROPHECY

Rosenthal and Jacobson (1968) in "Pygmalion in the classroom" describe an experiment, the Oak School Experiment, in which they administered what they referred to as the Harvard Test of Inflected Acquisition, a standard, non-verbal IQ test, to all students in a school located in a lower-class community. One-sixth of the school's population were Mexican children. The TOGA Test is a reasoning test which requires the child to match pictured items with verbal descriptions given by the teacher.

After students did the test, teachers were given a list of about twenty percent of the students picked at random and told that the test indicated that these children were expected to be potential spurters. All the children in the school were then retested with the same IQ test after one semester, after a full academic year, and after two full academic years.

"Expectancy advantage" was calculated by the degree to which IQ gains of the "special children" exceeded gains by children in the control group, i.e. those students who were not identified to teachers as "spurters." IQ tests administered after the first year indicated a significant expectancy advantage for children designated as "spurters," especially for children in the first and second grades. Children in the control group gained as well, but gains of children in the experimental group exceeded those of the students in the control group.[1]

Teacher expectation activates self-concept and breeds either success or failure, discipline or indiscipline (see appendix 3 for St. Paul's College experiment).

Paradoxically, even the success at examinations does not connote success in language ability, nor does failure in examinations connote language deficiency. The examination farce pressurizes both teacher and student into an explorative language context where tedious and dogmatic examination exercises are equated to a language arts program. The vicious circle continues because the ones who pass the examinations are the ones who will be teaching in the future, and to them success is in passing the examinations that they have passed. In this context, language teaching and language learning can never be enjoyed but must always be viewed as a serious pursuit of unattainable abstractions.

Examinations are generally geared not to test what we know but rather to test what we do not know. There are so many variables that shape the result of a language examination that success at an English examination may be determined by a matrix of dependable ranging from the inherent culture of the individual to the mood of the examiner. It is not uncommon for geniuses to be rejected and for mediocrity to flourish with As. The examination race has been responsible for more nervous breakdowns and sense of failure than it has served to attribute positive realization in society. But school and examinations also serve another disastrous non useful purpose—that of certifying failures.

In the school system, the apparently more brilliant students or sometimes the most docile ones are put in classes that are labeled better, and the supposedly less brilliant and sometimes the most vocal are put in another category labeled inferior. This categorization of men, whether as individuals or in groups, often generates more heat than light. The student in the inferior group has received his prophecy and has already been certified as failure. He has been told in no uncertain terms that he has failed is failing, and will fail. In the examination context, it is expected that only about 10 percent of the students will be successful. The global tragedy is that about 90 percent of the world's population leave school being told that they are failures, feeling to themselves that they are failures, and receiving a certificate to show that they have failed. Society accepts (or is it rejects?) them as such and they are absorbed into the milieu of the unsuccessful.

Ivan Illich discusses the problem in these terms:

Everywhere, all children know that they were given a chance, albeit an unequal one, in an obligatory lottery, and the presumed equality of the international standard now compounds their original poverty with the self-inflicted discrimination accepted by the dropout. They have been schooled to the belief in raising expectations and can now rationalize their growing frustration outside school by accepting their rejection from scholastic grace. They are excluded from heaven because once baptized, they did not go to church. Born in original sin, they are baptized into first grade, but to go Gehenna (which in Hebrew means "slum") because of their personal faults. As Max Weber traced the social effects of the belief that salvation belongs to those who accumulated wealth, we can now observe that grace is reserved for those who accumulate years in school.[2]

The teacher's perspective tends to be judgmental, irrational, and prejudicial. Judgmental because the teacher assigns social value to the child's language and finds him either a miscreant of a conformist; irrational because the judgement is not based on sound objectivity and understanding of the nature of linguistic development; and prejudicial because the teacher has set ideas about what constitutes proper language and evaluated the child's linguistic production relative to his own mould.

Teacher training has done little to nullify these misconceptions and the teacher training program is another arc in the wheel of misfortune that vicious circle of language learning and language teaching.

It may very well be that the input of language teachers has destroyed more creativity, disintegrated more humanity, frustrated more ability, and certified more failures than all the dialect speakers of the world combined.

NOTES

1. Kennard Ramphal, "An Analysis of Reading Instruction Offered to West Indian Creole-speaking Students" (Ph.D. diss., University of Toronto, 1983), 9-10.
2. Ivan Illich, *Deschooling Society* (New York: Harper and Row, 1983), 64.

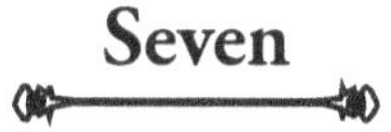

Seven

Illich on Deschooling*

Forgive them, for they know not what they teach.

Deschooling and more specifically "delanguage" teaching have scarcely been explored in literature. Ivan Illich, Paulo Freire, and others have introduced sociological phenomenology and deschooling in the education system, but this has not been applied to any specific subject area, only in general classroom situations.

Over the past few decades, however, much was said about dialectology, and in 1968 at the Mona campus at the University of the West Indies the first major conference was held in an effort to salvage Creole languages, thus enabling the eradication of linguistic apartheid. These efforts, however noble they might appear to be, are meagre attempts at a compromise when it comes to the classroom situation, and any repairs on the current system can only lead to more frustration. What linguists and teachers need to do is create for our present world a brandnew system of language sharing and language respect and dispense with the traditional concepts of language instruction and classroom manipulation.

*Page numbers in this chapter refer to Ivan Illich, Deschooling Society (New York: Harper and Row, 1983). In many instances language teaching is juxtaposed and liberal references are made.

At this point it is helpful if we can transfer the concepts of Illich's deschooling and relate them to the language teaching context. Ivan Illich opens his book by pointing out the confusion between learning and teaching and the institutionalization of teaching. This clearly juxtaposes the language arts programme. When teaching is finished in the classroom, where does the child really learn language? The classroom language simply serves the purpose of personal or selfish social class domination.

The world has for long existed on the fallacy that one has not learned language until and unless one has been schooled in it. The communication on the streets and among the dwellings of the poor (the meek and lowly) are relegated to the realm of nonlanguage, or in a more sympathetic tone, bad language. Society has cursed us with a social consciousness that does not recognise that language for the poor is different from language for the rich. Illich posits that since the middle class have access to education (and hence the language instruction program) they naturally perpetrate middle-class values. When a person from the working class or from a different geographical setting achieves the status of a language teacher, he is subjected to the ridicule and conditioning of the imposing forces and readjusts his linguistic performance to aspire to upper middle-class status. It becomes clear that language teaching has nothing to do with innate linguistic ability; it has only to do with social class control.

This is also revealed in the textbooks used in the classroom. For economic reasons the working class has little time to read and write so that publication of textbooks is largely the business of the middle class who would largely appeal to middle class values.

This infection develops psychological impotence on both sides— the oppressor and the oppressed because neither would share with the other his linguistic world.

Paulo Freire explains it this way:

> Yet it is —paradoxical though it may seem precisely the response of the oppressed to the violence of their oppressors that a gesture of love may be found. Consciously or unconsciously, the act of rebellion by the oppressed (an act which is always, or nearly always, as violent as the initial violence of the oppressors) can initiate love. Whereas the violence of the oppressors prevents the oppressed from being fully human, the response of the latter to this violence is grounded in the desire to pursue the right to be human. As

the oppressors dehumanized others and violate their rights, they themselves also become dehumanized. As the oppressed, fighting to be human, take away the oppressors' power to dominate and suppress, they restore to the oppressors the humanity they had lost in the exercise of oppression.

It is only the oppressed who, by freeing themselves, can free their oppressors. The latter, as an oppressive class, can free neither others nor themselves.[1]

The oppressor is not free because he is not free to love, not free to show kindness, not free to interact, and not free to learn. It is a strange paradox, but the slave is more free than the master. In the same way that Christ was more free than the Roman Empire the linguistic slave is more free than the language dominator. The "subordinate" is more free to learn and free to shift on the dialect continuum. This freedom of the oppressed is not always internalized because they develop a linguistic identity, yet operating fully consciously that they will never gain social acceptability. They sometimes even believe that they have some linguistic handicap. They are schooled into believing that "language of the poor" is synonymous with the language of the "dumb," and that this language has only entertainment value.

Again by juxtaposition, Illich suggests that the so-called linguistic (educational) disadvantage cannot be cured by relying on education within the school system. "Schools by their very structure resist the concentration of privilege on those otherwise disadvantaged. Special curricula, separate classes, or longer hours constitute more discrimination at a higher cost" (p. 8). Custodial care and reinforcement of degradation only serve to enhance the approach— you are not like us, you cannot speak as we do. The poor spend their money to be certified for the treatment of their alleged disproportionate linguistic deficiencies.

By inference, Illich further suggests that language teaching, rather than bringing together the linguistic variations in a community, polarizes the social differences and grades the nations of the world according to an international language system depending on which language has more currency.

It seems that the world is divided according to class, color, and codes and this pronounces the supposed deficiency of a specific social class.

Education for liberation in its truest sense has to do with the acceptance of peoples, cultures, and codes. There is, therefore, the immediate need to disestablish linguistic monopoly that carries with it prejudice, discrimination, mental torture, and control. The classroom has served to force students into an alien mode of thought and expression which consequently alienated the person from himself.

The language curriculum has always been used to assign social rank. At times it could be prenatal: Karma ascribes you to a caste and lineage to the aristocracy (p. 17). Your language seems preordained. School was meant to give everybody an equal chance to any office, but language teaching has categorized which chances are available to whom.

Increased language learning programs simply increase the destructiveness of these programs. Special language learning programs are like delinquent concentration camps, where the child interacts with other delinquents, but the camp makes them more rebellious to societal norms, so they become marginated from the linguistic paradigm of existence.

Illich purports that acceptance into a learning program presupposes competence in some other skill. Look at the simple paradox. Teachers are giving students language instructions in the first-person singular of the verb "to be," but the innate linguistic intricacies associated with the presentation and absorption of this concept are far more complex than "I am." Does this mean "I exist," or does it take a prepositional value such as, "I am here"? But the audacity goes further. Children are taught that their language is "inferior" in relation to the norm of a "better" language. The notion of universal correct English is mythological in a far greater sense than classical Greek mythology is. The fanaticism of the language teaching program in schools, the frequent mistakes in essays and the failures at the University of London G.C.E. examinations give enough proof that the current language arts programme in the Bahamas and similar developing countries has an antilinguistic, antieducational effect.

It is clear that normal children learn their first language casually, and that most people who learn a second language will do so as a result of odd circumstances, and not because of sequential teaching. Most people who read widely, and with pleasure merely believe that they learned to do so in school. When challenged, they easily discard this illusion (p. 18).

It therefore becomes necessary to dispel the confusion between learning and teaching. Language learning is always more effective through informal training and through contextual motivation. It is easier to learn journalism from a journalist at work and to learn the appropriate use of language wherever and whenever people use language. Most teachers are less communicative than the salesman or the ordinary man in the street.

The classroom relies on the arrangement of set circumstances which permit the learner to develop standard responses. This denies spontaneous creativity in language and negates the novel use of language. It is far more practical to develop partner relationship to communication and language usage. Paulo Friere shows how simple it is to learn language through social reality.

He discovered that any adult (in Brazil) can begin to read in a matter of forty hours if the first words he deciphers are charged with political meaning. Freire trains his teachers to move into a village and to discover the words which designate current important issues, such as the access to a well or the compound interest on the debts owed to the patron. In the evening the villagers meet for the discussion of these key words. They begin to realize that each word stays on the blackboard even after its sound has faded . . . (pp. 26-27).

The participation of the learner is crucial in the education process. Education for all means education by all. In the language arts programme all must participate, all must be respected, and we must not merely accommodate but give equal prominence to each dialect "standard" and "nonstandard." This involvement by all can be seen in rural societies where language and architecture and work and religion and family customs were consistent with one another, mutually explanatory and reinforcing. To grow into one implied a growth into others (p. 33).

The problem arises when we want to be censorious in an effort to avoid the "ignorant." Our imaginations are "all schooled up" and we share in the delusion that we can distinguish what is necessary language competence for others and what is not, just as former generations established laws which defined what was sacred and what was profane.

I have never heard of a situation where a ten-year-old native Spanish speaker taught a Spanish undergraduate in an English- speaking university. Yet the undergraduate has learned less Spanish at university than what the child has learned the first five years of his existence. But the university will insist that the child must be taught by the graduate and the same thing happens in our schools. English graduates are brought to teach English in the Bahamas and they do not care about what the children know or what the children can teach them.

Language instruction, therefore, becomes a process in de-humanizing childhood.

Everyone learns to live outside of school. We learn to speak, to think, to love, to feel, to play, to curse, to politic, and to work without interference from a teacher (p. 42). In fact the teacher obstructs language learning in school. The conversations of interest that lend themselves to creativity are curtailed when the teacher steps in the classroom. Only recently (1986) at Saint Paul's College an eighth grade student, in his essay, described the male genitals as "cowbells." He was disciplined for obscenity by his English language instructor. Yet one must admit that it takes a great deal of creativity to use such figurative language.

Teachers also obstruct learning in assigning to students the self-fulfilled prophecy. Some students are told that they use too much dialect and as a result are put in set three, where they do not have a chance at proving themselves (see appendix 4). The lamentable phenomenon is that many schools in the Bahamas bring teachers from abroad to tell the children how "dumb" they are and to infer that the children have a cultural and linguistic inferiority. It is a "crying shame" that school raises the hopes of the children that even if they are not successful, one day their grandchildren will learn to speak proper English. This emasculation of the dialect is a denial of one's very existence.

The child and his perception of reality is through his native language, and the omniscient role of the teacher disallows and imprisons this expression. The child is "educated" in the scholastic womb of irrelevance, and at graduation is delivered into the world to begin life all over again.

The idea that one person's judgement should determine when and what another person must learn has given rise to many countercultures. Almost every counterculture has developed its own peculiar linguistic code, because it is only through language that they are free to think and to shape and explain the world of their existence. Their consciousness of reality becomes different as they induce linguistic novelty in their communication.

Illich discusses school in terms of the myth of unending consumption and infers that learning can exist without the language arts programme but once formal education in language instruction has begun, it produces the illusionary demand for more and better language instruction. No one stops to even consider that the quest for puritanism in language is the chasing of a mirage and that language is basically self-taught. Once the self-taught man or woman has been discredited, all nonprofessional activity is rendered suspect.

We need to stretch our imagination to the limit to believe that language competence can be measured and documented by grades and certificates. Language learning is an activity that needs the least manipulation by others. It is rather the result of unhampered participation in a meaningful setting.

Under the heading "The Myth of Measurement of Values," Illich posits that "School initiates young people into a world where everything can be measured, including their imaginations, and indeed, man himself" (p. 57). A child's language competence can never be measured because language is such an intrinsic matter. One can attempt to evaluate his performance, but then there are ideological differences between any two speakers of the same language, so to rate one person in relation to another is unreasonable. We cannot expect people to go around mimicking other people's speech, besides even to expect this is to infringe on the right of the individual.

The language arts programme has inducted students into "the ritual of rising deception" and serves as a force of alienation by the institutionalization of the word of life simply by teaching the need to be taught. Once this lesson is learned people lose linguistic innovation and creativity, which alone can bring them out of oppression into independence. By communication they will begin to find their relatedness attractive and will be open to the surprises which life offers. "Delanguage" teaching will enable them to shake off the institutionalized manipulation of man's world shaped by his language. The oppressive linguistic pedagogy embraces a belief that man can do what God cannot, namely, manipulate others for their own salvation. It may very well be that this inflicted complex has been responsible for very few geniuses and inventions in so-called third world countries because language implicitly and explicitly shapes our cosmos and conditions our thoughts, and there are many people going around who are afraid to think because they feel uncomfortable with their native language.

Every language arts teacher perceives himself as a speech therapist, whose ministrations all men need, and when the educator and educate realize that they both have languages, a classroom of chaos emerges. In this mutual frustration both blame money, time, building, or eventually they turn on one another to lay blame for the failure. Administrators tend to blame the teacher- training programme. But can one really teach a teacher how to teach? Can an institution imbue him with the feeling that teaching is an act of love and mercy?

Aristotle speaks of this as a "moral type of friendship," which is not on fixed terms: it makes a gift, or does whatever it does, as a friend. This kind of teaching is always a luxury for the teacher and a form of leisure (in Greek *schole*) for him and his pupil: an activity meaningful for both, having no ulterior purpose" (p. 46).

"Delanguage" teaching will offer to the world a new and fresh vision of reality as long as we are prepared to respect national, regional, dialectal, and ideolectal differences. Through language we will learn to understand one another and love one another and "Lift the human race above and beyond the fear, ignorance and isolation which beset it today" (p. 169).

NOTES

1. Paulo Freire, *Pedagogy of the Oppressed* (New York: Seabury Press, 1968), 41-42.

Eight

Dialectology—the Universal Paradigm

These speak evil of those things which they know not.
                              —Epistle of Jude

Attitudes to dialects have been mentioned in chapter 3, where Dell Hymes noted the stigma of dialects. He made it clear, however, that this "stepchild" may very well prove a Cinderella.

The Bahamas share with six million people in and around the Caribbean not merely similar linguistic problems, but the same linguistic problem. Linguists who examine the historicity and development of dialects have proposed several theories.

Paul Bloomfield and others developed several polygenetic theories which generally reduce the dialect to a subordinate and dependent language. David Decamp explains: "Each speaker deliberately mutilated the standard language by eliminating all grammatical inflections, reducing the number of phonological and syntactic contrasts, and limiting the vocabulary to a few hundred words. The resulting structure was described by many scholars as a 'corruption,' a 'minimum grammar, a return to an 'archaic state.'[1]

Taylor, Whinnon, and others develop the monogenetic theory of the development of Pidgin and Creole languages and pointed out that the similarities of these languages are too great for simple coincidence: "William Stewart (1962) discussed the functions of structure and lexicon in linguistic relationships and concluded that the divergent relexification (i.e. a wholesale shift of vocabulary) of a single proto-pidgin was a more tenable hypothesis than the convergent restructuring of a whole group of separate languages."[2]

It is also possible that there was a combination of both theories in the evolution of Pidgins and Creoles (I must give credit to George Cave at the University of Guyana for this opinion).

Whatever the reality is, the monogenetic theory has merits on two counts. Firstly, they would have us think of an Anglicized Creole rather than Creolized English in the Bahamian context. This is crucial because the combination of words would condition our thought and reaction. Creolized English suggests a degeneration and corruption of the standard adopted by those unable to speak the standard. Now we know that this cannot be true because any person has the innate ability to speak any language that he grows up into. The Creolized English theory suggests that the poorer and darker members of the society are incapable of speaking the Queen's English, and in an effort to do their best, they end up with a base form of the language which we call the dialect.

To speak of Anglicized Creole, however, is to suggest that the Creole existed before English lexical items were added to it. Whinnon suggests that Sabir, the lingua franca of the Mediterranean, was the protocreole. A wholesale process of relexification occurred and this resulted in the type of Anglicised Creole we have in the Bahamas. This gives the Creole a different status and we begin to understand it, not as a corruption but as a synthesis of linguistic development. Some researchers even claim that at one time the planters were learning Creole language from the slaves. Others have found a significant trace of West African language in Caribbean Creoles.

The second useful purpose of the monogenetic theory is to historize in a unique and unified way the existence of Creole cultures. Dell Hymes propounds: "Their very existence is largely due to the process-discovery, exploration, trade, conquest, slavery, migration, colonialism, nationalism— that have brought the peoples of Europe and the peoples of the rest of the World to share a common destiny. "3

In a recent study by grade eleven students at Saint Paul's College, a field trip was made to determine the following: (a) the extent of the Creole in Grand Bahama; and (b) the context of Creole usage (see appendix 5). This group found that the Bahamian Creole exists quite freely where there is no interference of a stranger and it seems that the Bahamian Creole is mutually intelligible to Jamaican Creole, Guyanese Creole, and other Anglicized Creoles in the region. The students also found that though they were native Bahamians and approached informants in dialect, informants felt shy and reluctant (and may even feel insulted) to respond in dialect. They were more willing to show their knowledge of things than to relax and respond in the natural dialect. A great deal of persuasion was necessary to get Creole responses.

The responses generally depended on the subject matter discussed. When informants were discussing the native culture or an event that excited them, they tended to be more unguarded and to speak more naturally in dialect.

I point these out not merely to prove the existence of a Bahamian Creole, but also to explain that this Creole exists in what is perceived to be a subculture of the people. It must be sounded loud and clear that this is not the subculture but the real culture—the prominent and predominant culture of the Bahamian people—and that other imposed and adapted cultures exist, but on the fringes of the real existence of the people. What this field trip has put into focus is that people arc afraid of what others might think them to be if they use Bahamian dialect.

We shall now discuss the way Creoles are treated universally-some pseudolinguists have represented Creole languages as "the blind groping of minds too primitive for expressions in modes of speech beyond their capabilities."[4] Originally, young linguists were advised not to waste time on such unimportant subjects, but to study real languages if they wish to get on in the academic world. Creoles are seen as marginated languages spoken by a marginated people who are excluded from the normal life of society. Their communication was seen as linguistically insufficient and so they cannot qualify for admission into real society.

DeCamp makes thc point that "A Creole is inferior to its corresponding standard language only in social status." This social status is assigned generally by an education programme that refuses to tolerate the dialect among those who are "schooled" or learned. They are so schooled up that they cannot see it differently and regard the dialect as an opportunity for amusement, and the dialect speakers as objects of amusement. Recognition of the dialect is also a political and economic decision, since politics and economics determine what is the standard language of the community. DeCamp made an important observation as far as politics, economics, and education are concerned.

"If the equivalent European language is also the standard language of the community, the Creole is especially unlikely to be granted status as a real language. Rather it is thought of as merely a barbarous corruption of the standard language:

In Jamaica, for example, most educators persist in treating the "dialect problem" as if it were a problem of speech correction, attributing it to careless, slovenly pronunciation. The few exceptional teachers who see it as a foreign-language problem (or a quasi-language problem) are considered dangerously radical by many Jamaicans. The Creole is inseparably associated with poverty, ignorance, and lack of moral character. This association is, of course, a half truth, for the poor, the uneducated, and the unambitious do speak the broader varieties of Creole, whereas the bright young boy with a chance at education and a white-collar job strives diligently to acquire the Kingston middle-class standard. However, it is the social prejudice against Creole which is partially responsible for continued poverty, ignorance, and lack of ambition. The overwhelming majority of the population are told every day of their lives that they will never amount to anything because they talk Quashie,' and the nouveau-riche superiority of their own "standard" English while nursing inward doubts about whether their English is really sufficiently standard. The written compositions of school children are dull and vapid because the children are so fearful of lapsing into their native Creole that they cannot express themselves freely."[5]

If there is to be any kind of linguistic liberation in Creole communities like the Bahamas, it is imperative that the Creole be given prominent social status; but more so that dialect speakers discover with pride the music and complexity of their language and they must be prepared to use this language creatively. The stigma of dropping inflectional endings is irrational because certainly the English language does not have as many infectional endings as Spanish or French but that does not make English an inferior language.

NOTES

1. David DeCamp, "Introduction the Study of Pidgin and Creole Languages," in Pidginization and Creolization of Languages, ed. Dell Hymes (London: Cambridge University Press, 1971), 19. All extracts from this book are reprinted by permission of Cambridge University Press.
2. Ibid., 23.
3. Hymes, Pidginization and Creolization of Languages, 5.
4. Ibid., 4.
5. DeCamp, "Introduction," 26.

Nine

Dialectology and Language Teaching

There is nothing evil in itself—thinking makes it so.

From bidialectism in the United States to bilingualism in smaller Creole-speaking countries we have gone a long way in confusing the issue of dialect in the classroom. The creation of the Creole continuum by reputed linguists bears inherently a notion of standardization which the nonstandard speaker must aim at, lest he be certified as a societal reject, and hence of lesser intelligence.

The simple paradox in this situation is that these same linguists will tell you that the standard language is, in fact, a standard dialect and that the idea of superiority of any dialect above another is purely mythical. The question, therefore, is redundant. "Why must we teach some sort of 'standard English'?" Even professional linguists like Dennis Craig would make a claim that the newly emerging English-speaking West Indian nations "face social and educational problems directly attributable to the fact that forms of English Creole speech are the everyday language of the majority of their populations."[1]

The so-called problems referred to by Dennis Craig are not real problems but created problems—problems created in order to foster a linguistic hierarchy that will doctor the present educational system and increase spending to destroy more language and more people. I refer to these as *created problems* because no basilectal speaker goes around having problems in communicating. If their language is as important as the middle-class standard and the middle class is acclaimed more intelligent (because they can monopolize language production) then why doesn't the middle-class person make the effort to learn the language of basilect? After all, the more intelligent should be more versatile.

The ignorance and absurdity continues in one of Bailey's comments: "It is possible to move from one social class to another by changing one's linguistic norm. This is of course due to another factor, the correlation between a good education and acceptable English, which makes it possible to assume that ability to manipulate SJE (Standard Jamaican English) is indicative of a good education, in addition of course, to birth in higher caste or class."[2]

Paulo Freire states unequivocally that education serves a purpose for either domestication or liberation. Education cannot be neutral. Yet the perpetrating of a so-called accepted middle- class standard code as opposed to one that is unacceptable and nonstandard is to politicize language teaching and to foster authoritarian principles which result in segregation, prejudice, and margination within the classroom and the society. It is most dangerous in language teaching because the child is not allowed to think in his native language and we label him "dumb" because he finds it difficult to think in an alien language.

If we are really seeking an egalitarian classroom, then there must be participation by all, and students must be allowed to construct for themselves a critical relationship with reality. Concepts of acceptability and standardization cannot be handed down to them like the antique papal bull. They have to be allowed to question and criticize accepted norms and the very existence of these norms. Each individual student must be allowed to actively create for himself a world relevant to his own existence.

In 1982, I agreed with George Cave when he wrote: "In the context of Guyana, however, I make the claim that the major factor influencing the production of standard language is the Creolese dialects present in the society. I claim that almost every error made in the language of the children we teach can be traced to Creolese interference or to hypercorrection which themselves are affected by a matrix of interfacing forces."[3]

Now I disagree profusely with the very suggestion of Cave's statement. *Error* is not an absolute term, but is a relative term that reflects only human choices and, in many instances, human degradation on the part of those who founded the linguistic errors. The linguist has now taken the omniscient role of assigning linguistic sins to the student and ascertaining the relative punishments. I object to any suggestion that error is associated with any dialect or made as a result of a dialect not accepted in the classroom. In fact when the student uses a different dialect in the classroom, it is not the student on trial but it puts the teacher on trial. It is then when we see all the prejudice of the teacher coming out— his ignorance, his cultural biases, his inability to accommodate a different point of view, his aspirations toward middle class, his rejection of the working class (in many instances his roots), and his lack of strength and courage to protect and foster his cultural roots and truly liberating education.

Indeed, as Dennis Craig points out:

> The societies in all territories are, in a way, trapped within their standard English traditions; widespread inability to use the standard language is resulting in increasing wastage in expanding educational systems, a wastage which poor economies cannot afford. Official government statements in all territories; apart from putting increasing emphasis on the social-mobility value of English and condemning school examination results (which often give a failure rate at all levels of between 60-85% in English in most territories) show very little insight into the real nature of the problem.[4]

Wittingly or unwittingly, Dennis Craig has so aptly used the verb *trapped*, because that seems to be the whole purpose of the school's language-teaching program—to trap people within some unreal and unattainable language traditions. Delanguage teaching offers liberation from this trap and exposes the indecency associated with it.

Again, Dennis Craig refers to the wastage resulting from this linguistic trap. It is all well and good to recognize the trap, but the way to escape is not by spending more money to improve a system that is responsible for trapping all of us. It is like attempting to reform people by building more jails, whereas, the real reformation needs to be done at the heart of society. James Sledd puts it this way: "Government and the foundations began to spray money over the academic landscape like liquid fertilizer, and the professional societies began to bray and paw at the rich new grass. In that proud hour, any teacher who could dream up an expensive scheme for keeping things as they were while pretending to make a change was sure of becoming the director of a project . . . . [5]

In an effort to upgrade the language of speakers of so-called non-standard dialect (which incidentally Sledd described as turning lower-class trash into middle-class trash), many schools of linguistics have been busy producing pattern drills and some dare to claim success that after a week of intense drills the child no longer says "tree man is swimin" but instead, would say "three men are swimming." The English teacher will not stop to think that both are understood by the society nor would he be able to determine the amount and depth of psychological and sociological damage done to the student. Many times, the frustrated child will ever after be afraid to even think of three men swimming, and will definitely not speak about it again if it can be avoided.

This is why many students perceive the world of the class room as an existence divorced from the world of reality. "Three men are swimming" is by the classroom and for the classroom, but it has absolutely no relevance to when they get to the beach—except that it may send a small tinge of fear if they do see three men swimming in the sea. Maybe this is why there is so much disinterest and even open rebellion in the classroom setting. The students cannot bring the world of their reality, the world of their thoughts, dreams, and emotions, into the classroom because when one enters that sacred domain, he/she has to stop thinking in dialect.

Sociolinguist Basil Bernstein emphasizes the relationship between language and perception: "Language is considered one of the most important means of initiating, synthesizing, and reinforcing ways of thinking, feeling, and behaviour which are functionally related to the social group."[6]

Recent literary critics discuss at length the problem of identity (or lack of it) overshadowing West Indian literature. Even our great writers seem to have their perception of themselves and their society all schooled up. Works of art or any creativity must be measured in terms of the standard linguistic trap, and if the only linguistic tools you have available are "standard" forms, then it becomes impossible to initiate or synthesize one's own concept if that person's modus operandi is a different dialect. It is this linguistic consciousness that affects the verbalization of feeling in the child. Bernstein further submits that "the word mediates between the expression of feeling and its approved social recognition, that is, a value is placed upon the verbalization of feelings."[7] This can be one of the reasons why children in schools are afraid to "speak out in class," because "they feel with different words than those which they are compelled to use in class"—the word at this point ceases to be the word of life and becomes uncompromisingly the word of death.

Many linguists have recognized the conflict of dialects in the classroom but they tend to describe the problem as one of nonstandard dialect in the classroom. It seems as if the problem is never with this "standard" dialect and the way teachers present it—it is never with the superimposition of our own cultural or linguistic biases. It is always with the poorer (and sometimes darker) members of the society and the language that they are associated with.

With time comes progress, as James Britton points out:

> Amongst other recommendations it [a document on language teaching] warned teachers to draw a sharp distinction between the language of the home and the street and the language the school is trying to achieve. And it went as far as to suggest that teachers should not set children to talk or write about their homes or neighborhoods because that would be inviting them to use the wrong language. There are plenty of teachers in our various countries who still operate a 'fresh start' policy for language in their classrooms. But we have made some advances in fifty years: no official statement would dare to put forward so linguistically naive and ignorant a view today."[8]

He sees our current way of teaching as a way of drawing people away from their roots and cultures, rather than a way of increasing their activities within those groups and cultures.

V. K. Edwards therefore advised us that "the soundest approach to the teaching of standard English is to show that different dialects are accepted and appreciated by the school. For it is not until a child is a competent user of his own linguistic system that standard English will cease to be a threat." The statement concludes by saying that it is necessary for the child to receive his early education in his natural vernacular.[9]

Of course these are traditional educators and they will all see the need for a language teaching program in the education system. What is surprising is that they all know the value of the vernacular but still have as the carrot in front upward social mobility and some form of standard English. It is like giving absolution to a person because he knows the evil that he was doing was evil.

Some linguists try to breathe life into the dying cause for a language teaching program. McLeod makes this concession: "Even if this distinction could be made, it might be wise to defer the correction of the dialect forms until the writer knows what is dialect and what is standard in the sentence in question."[10] He implies that it is psychologically unsound to ridicule a student who just has an alternative way of saying the same thing. The pointing out of the "mistakes" (though it damages the self-concept of the child) encourages him to use a more socially accepted alternative. This premise can be used to establish a case for bidialectalism in the Bahamian language teaching context.

It would be very meritorious at this point to ask, "Why must the child be taught to want to use a form of middle-class language if the child is not of that particular social stratum?" If liberating education is to be education for the masses, then it is their language and their culture that must be predominant in educational pursuits. A political decision, however, to accept vernacular in the classroom will shatter the middle-class monopoly, and it is they who largely control politics and education. They would lose their control over people, and their claim to better education and higher intelligence will dissipate like the morning dew. The linguistic aristocrats will find themselves running around in the "Emperor's New Clothes" but no one will be there to tell them how beautiful it looks.

The middle-class monopoly is simply this: "If you talk like us, you are one of us, and if you talk like them, then you are stupid, dumb, and inferior." In the words of Sledd, "the great purpose of the language-teaching program is to teach the under- dogs, middle dog barking." The dialect speaker is always a setback in the classroom. He/she is perceived as a bad influence on the middle-class child, and the paradox is that the middle-class child enthusiastically learns the dialect because in it he finds some social acceptance. He wakes up out of the middle-class nightmare of standard English but the teacher in the classroom is a constant reminder of his standardized nightmare and he is constantly drawn back into bondage despite his efforts to break loose from it. Students are finding that the way to rebel against the linguistic oppression is by discovering and initiating their use of nonstandard dialect and the language of "rebel" cultures.

It is this dialect that offers to the student a kind of salvation that human beings long most for—the need to be recognized as an individual, to be accepted, to be approved, and to be loved. It is in this linguistic mode that he discovers a beautiful world of sharing, of life, of beauty, of creativity, and of expression. And the classroom denies him the world of this existence.

The student constantly faces the threat of the imposition of an alien standard, the eradication of his "substandard," and of himself. Fortunately, as James Sledd opines: "The English teacher's forty-five minutes a day for five days in the week will never counteract the influence, and sometimes the hostility, of playmates and friends and family during much the larger part of the student's time."[11]

Rudine Sims of the University of Massachusetts in an experiment in reading shows that the dialect does not have a serious impact on the ability to read standard English. The responsibility for the student's inability to read is squarely placed on the shoulders of the teacher, and pedagogy is the scapegoat chosen on this occasion. No time was devoted to discuss the material that is offered to test the students' reading ability. I can make a fool of the most brilliant linguists if I have them participate in a reading test which describes the preparation of the "conch" (pronounced "konk" in the Bahamas) from the shell to conch chowder. When the students are asked to read about totally unfamiliar experiences or objectionable experiences associated with middle-class domination and middle-class ideas, it does not take a genius to predict what the results will be. Anyone can get the results he/she set out to get— just gear the test accordingly. The real problem for "dialect" speakers is that the material provided is lathered with unfamiliar images and the child is fully aware that he is asked to attempt to read like someone else, to imitate the oppressor, and to parrot someone else's speech, and this is a further process in the dehumanization of student hood.

Not only is the child dehumanized, but the teacher is more dehumanized because it is subhuman to reject a person for who he is. The student is dehumanized only to the extent that his self-concept is shattered and he is embarrassed because he does not speak like someone else.

The student is made to be a patient who needs linguistic doctoring and is a burden to society because more money has to be spent on curing his disability. He is discreet enough to want to reject this expensive treatment, because he really does not feel sick, but he is trapped. The teacher (the linguistic doctor), his future employers, and the society at large makes it very clear to him that if he rejects the treatment he will die—at least, socially and academically. No doubt, many traditional educators will look at the dialectal window dressing and praise the educational system for the charitable concessions made in giving some cognisance to the substandard dialect of the subhuman.

Ira Shore makes the point "when I think of my dream for society, I see liberating education for something and education against something."[12] The education in the classroom is explicitly for middle-class "standard" English and all the values and thoughts associated with this language and against the language of the working class—the labeled nonstandard or substandard dialect. If language is an indication of thought, then these "subhumans" must have had a very difficult time thinking. Language teaching cannot be neutral.

The recognition of the different idiolects in the classroom would also give rise to more dialogue and participation in the linguistic education process. Experience and meaningful involvement will replace the "monologue of the talking teacher who lectures students into silence and boredom."

Maybe the greatest illusion in dialectology and language teaching is the myth that you do not need to pay much attention to the dialect. Just ignore it, reinforce standard usage, and eventually the dialect will disappear. This is not only false security but it is false security of a very ignorant and arrogant kind. And this is why minor concessions of the recognition of dialect in the classroom is not good enough. What is needed is not improved conditions but total liberation. The falsity that we do not need linguistic liberation hides the grossness of the hundreds of years of suffering and pain associated with middle-class values of linguistic inequalities and incompetence. The language teaching program in the classroom is among the worst kind of child abuse that has gone on for so long that we have developed a numbness to the reality. Children have been negated of everything that means anything to them their language, their existence, and their reality. If students are to become active creators of meaning and develop a critical relationship with reality, nothing short of delanguage teaching will suffice.

NOTES

1. Dell Hymes, ed., *Pidginization and Creolization of Languages* (London: Cambridge University Press, 1971), 371.

2. Ibid., 374.

3. Dwarka Ramphal, "The Teaching of Tense and Agreement at Covent Garden Secondary School" (Dip. Ed. thesis, University of Guyana, 1971), 7.

4. Hymes, *Pidginization and Creolization*, 375-76.

5. James Sledd, "Didialectalism: The Linguistics of White Supremacy," *English Journal*, 1969, 1308.

6. Basil Bernstein, *Class Codes and Control-Theoretical Studies towards a Sociology of Languages*, vol. 1 (London: Routledge and Kegan Paul, 1973), 43.

7. Ibid., 25.

8. James Britton, "English Teaching: Retrospect and Prospect," *English*

9. *in Education* 15, no. 2 (Summer 1981), 1. 9. V. K. Edwards, "The West Indian Language Issue in British Schools," Language in Society 9, no. 3 (December 1980), 400.

10. A. McLeod, "Writing Dialect and Linguistic Awareness," English in Education 15, no. 2, 26.

11. Sledd, "Didalectalism," 1313.

12. Rachel Martin, "A Conversation with Ira Shore," *Literary Research Center 2*, no. 1 (Spring 1986).

Ten

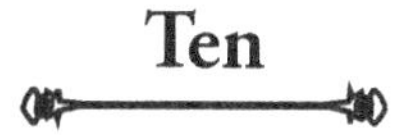

The Language of Oppression

Dumb dogs that cannot bark.
                    —Isaiah 56:10

From Fanon to Freire, the central theme is the language of liberation. Whole continents, whole cultures, whole languages, and whole peoples are engulfed by a monstrosity under the guise of civilization. "We taught them to speak, to wear shirts and dresses," is the absurd claim of these so-called apostles of light. We killed them and reduced them to children of silence is the reality of this confrontation.

Inherently, the colonised, the slave, or the indentured servant knows that he has a language and that he should be free to speak his dialect without the need to feel less than a man. And that is exactly what the coloniser would like to deny him. "We can't understand you when you speak, you're too dumb, you're too stupid." This is the remnant of colonial heritage to make people feel inferior when they want to say something. The one-time colonies of the great empire have broken away from political and economic domination. The subtle linguistic domination, however, under the pretense of nice-sounding words like *education, culture*, and prestige, persists in a tyrannical manner. It is difficult to break out of it because it is not even recognised.

The leaders of the now-free colonies assert independence in all kinds of spontaneous and sometimes erratic ways. In most cases it simply boils down to replacing one set of masters by another set of masters who do nothing but mimic the old ones. The whole affair is like a monkey revolution and the wheel has gone full circle—we have completed a revolution; we have ended just where we started.

In the Bahamas, the hysterical insistence on the teaching and learning of standard British English is most oppressive at best. Government ministers, high school principals, and so many others have the feeling that they have to fly to London to recruit English teachers. If one speaks with a West Indian accent, he or she is not good enough for the Bahamas, as far as some prominent politicians are concerned. The wounds of colonialism are hurting us everyday, only this time we press the daggers in our own bosoms.

Maybe it is the only way that the new leaders can maintain a semblance of social supremacy. They pull out their credit card, which reads: "I have been schooled in London; I have heard the Queen's English." When people (the liberated masses) begin to say, "But that doesn't tell us anything, you are not running the country the way we want to," the politicians submerge themselves in the illusion of a superiority complex. Like Alice in Wonderland they tell the electorates, "If you want to make a point, make it in standard English because the country is an English-speaking country." If a champion of the masses should say that "When we use a word it means what we want it to mean, because we are the society," that is looked upon with great suspicion and regarded with mistrust. If his language cannot be silenced, then the extreme alternative is to silence his voice totally.

The oppressed worker is not deluded by high-sounding phrases and fancy words. He knows that he is strong and healthy and that he is a man, regardless of what his oppressor wants him to believe. He knows that his identity and the identities of all his children are wrapped in their language. It is through this language that they exist, perceive their existence, explain their existence, and will pass the future of their existence to their children. The perception of reality, of the oppressed and oppressor, of the neutrality of the landscape and the sea, of the massification of his society are all integrated in his language. No wonder then that his dominators want to deny him his language.

In the days gone by when his foreparents had not yet achieved emancipation, their language of freedom and of reality was the language of the body and language of the drum. Then the goatskin spoke with a shrill challenge of freedom and the body resisted every touch of the whip and every command of the master. Today, under the pretext of civilization, we have lost the language of the drum and have rejected the language of our people. We speak but we are ashamed to speak because they will laugh at us and they will say we are dumb and stupid. They do not want to hear what we have to say; they only want to laugh at us when we speak. Maybe the United Nations Human Rights charter should adopt a new section which gives everyone the right to speak and the right to be listened to. Mental anguish suffered by whole communities which have had authoritarian impositions is paralleled only by wholesale murder and torture of whole communities.

Colonizers, if they succeed in castrating the language of the colonised and give potency to their own language in that community, have succeeded in subjecting the colony. Jean-Paul Sartre puts it this way: "The European elite undertook to manufacture a native elite. They picked out promising adolescents; they branded them as with a red-hot iron, with the principles of Western culture; they stuffed their mouths full with high-sounding phrases, grand, glutinous words that stuck to the teeth. After a short stay in the mother country they were sent home, whitewashed."[1]

The process of dehumanizing, therefore, is to create a dream (elusive though it is) of adopting the tongue of the mother country. It is, in practice, the rejection of one's own mother in preference for a foster mother. This is done by presenting to the child the notion that the foster mother is richer, wiser, more powerful, and has a better language— "the language of progress." His natural mother, however, is poor, incompetent, under cultured, and speaks the language of regression.

Those who reject this absurdity are relegated to the ranks of nonhuman. If one persists in speaking the language of the natives, the colonizers will have him rejected, many times by his own people. The aim is to make the strong-willed believe that he is not human enough and so "everything will be done to wipe out their [native] traditions, to substitute our [colonizer] language for theirs and to destroy their culture without giving them ours."[2]

This experience is a very traumatic experience. It is very shattering to wake up one morning to find out that the language you have taught your children for so many years is not a real language because they say it is not written or it is not spoken by some monarch in some place far away. You wake up to the notion that you have perceived the world incorrectly because your incorrect language cannot possibly allow you to perceive the world in its correctness. The mere fact that this is the way your parents and fore parents perceived and interpreted the universe seems relatively unimportant. The stranger now shapes words and thought "the very forms of organization of the struggle will suggest to him [the colonized] a different vocabulary. *Brother, sister, friend—* these are words outlawed by the colonialist bourgeoisie because for them my brother is my purse, my friend is a part of my scheme for getting on."[3] Fanon makes no claim to being a linguist but his linguistic insight is very significant even today. He writes for the third world, the "subculture," the "subhuman" and the speaker of the substandard dialect and his message is one of being human.

The linguistic phenomenon in liberation dialectics has been largely overlooked by both linguists and the liberation philosophers. Yet the inferences of language control are so vivid that they are difficult to miss. It is easy to control the body but difficult to control the thought. Yet, if one can control language, the tool of thought, one can control the shape of a person's thought. Think yes, think master, think obey, the brainwashing exercise of man's inhumanity to other men. Fanon continues: "In fact, the terms the settler uses when he mentions the native are sociological terms. He speaks of the yellow man's reptilian motions, of the stink of the native quarter, of breeding swarms, of foulness, of spawn, of gesticulations. When the settler seeks to describe the native fully in exact terms he constantly refers to the bestiality."[4]

Sekou Toure says: "To take part in the African revolution it is not enough to write a revolutionary song; you must fashion it with the people, the songs will come by themselves, and of themselves."[5]

Fanon agrees with him: "For these individuals, the demand for national culture and the affirmation of the existence of such a culture represent a special battlefield. "[6]

The growth of a culture, of an identity, of a reality, and of a meaningful existence is imperative if the oppressed is to have any kind of liberating experience. The foundation of all culture, song, creativity, and perception is the language that one speaks, and education is a major determining factor in how much respect is allocated to the dialect. The removal of educational and social oppression demands "no less than a complete demolishing of all existing structures." Those who are fearful of the critical consciousness of the people must reassess themselves in the light that all language and all people are equal.

NOTES

1. Frantz Fanon, *The Wretched of the Earth* (New York: Grove Press, 1968), preface.
2. Ibid., preface.
3. Ibid., 47.
4. Ibid., 42.
5. Ibid., 206.
6. Ibid., 207.

Eleven

Pedagogy of the Oppressed

Give me words and I will blind your God.
—Edward Braithwaite

The title of this chapter is borrowed from Paulo Freire's book, *Pedagogy of the Oppressed*, and in it he states:

> Education is suffering from narration sickness. His [the teacher's] task is to "fill" the student with the contents of his narration contents which are detached from reality, disconnected from the totality that endangered them and could give them significance. Words are emptied of their concreteness and become hollow, alienated, and alienating verbosity. The outstanding characteristic of this narrative education, then, is the sonority of words, not their transforming power.[1]

Though Freire never claims to be a linguist, yet his linguistic insights would stagger the feeble attempts of trained linguists who try to prop up a language-teaching system that has failed, is failing, and it will fail because it has no bearing on the real existence of human beings. It is of this shattering truism that we are really afraid and because we are afraid that the frailty of our security will crumble, we hold tenaciously to our dreams of seeming reality. Hence, there can be no real liberation because we are afraid to liberate ourselves from the clutches of dogma and tradition.

The pedagogy practiced in the classroom today is first of all a pedagogy of ignorance. Pit Corder, a leading British linguist, and author of several books on applied linguistics, emphasizes the point that,

Language is a very complex thing, and it cannot yet be fully accounted for by anyone within one wholly consistent and comprehensive theory. Certainly, linguists have found it so. For this reason, when asked the question what is language, the linguist is likely to reply by another question: "Why do you want to know?" If we teach language, the way we approach our task will be influenced, or even determined, by what we believe language to be, by the particular informal theory or theories we have about it which seem to be relevant to the particular problem we are faced with.[2]

It is very rare that we find such an honest confession from an expert, but I hope that Corder is prepared to accept the implications of this statement. If language is so intricate that we cannot understand how it works then is it not a logical conclusion to posit that language teachers have been ploughing through the maze of ignorance for a very long time? It further suggests that nothing is wrong with the students, but something may be wrong with the teacher and with those who insist on the language teaching program.

Pit Corder tries to rationalize this tradition of ignorance by suggesting that we approach language teaching according to what we perceive language to be. The problem is, however, that if we are honest or we are truly liberated we would know with absolute certainty that we do not know what language is. What most teachers do at this point of confusion is that they realize that they have to do something to retain their job, to receive their salaries, and maintain their dependants so they will not dare to challenge the status quo. The teacher, therefore, conjures some imagination of what he thinks language should be believed to be, and conforms as closely as possible to what was done by his predecessors.

Language exists in the same way that thought exists. They both exist wherever man exists. Thought is individualistic. Language is gregarious and societal. Both thought and language exist intuitively and inherently in mankind. Maybe it will be absurd for me to suggest that we should introduce a new subject in the classroom—let us call it "thinkology." In this class we teach students how to think, because you need to use thought in every other subject and in every area of existence. I am certain there will be many objections, such as "students learn to think in every class," "you cannot teach people to think, they have to be born with it," "you cannot teach people to think in a vacuum, there has to be something to think about," and many others. I submit that every objection also holds true for the language-teaching program.

There is much futility and ignorance associated with the language-teaching program as it exists today and it is this exercise in futility and ignorance that makes the whole program oppressive on the national budget, on the school, on the teacher, and especially on the student. As far as language teaching is concerned classroom pedagogy is also misleading. It presents a feeling that we have so much data on language—after all everyone in high school can speak and say what he or she wants to say—but does not recognize that it is virtually impossible to "exteriorize" this data, or in Chomsky's terminology, to achieve a "psychic distance" from what we are studying.

Pit Corder posits: "Nevertheless, the achievement of 'psychic distance' is by no means easy, not even for linguists. All too frequently, linguists, like language teachers, make statements or assumptions based, not on objective study, but on intuitive 'private' knowledge."[3] How often does a teacher say that such a word is never used in a particular context? Has he based this statement on his, or another's objective research? Such private intuitions, for the unwary, may be easily expressed in prescriptive form or as value judgements. When someone asserts "People don't say that," is this a statement of fact, the truth of which can be demonstrated, or is it really a value judgement? Does it really mean that it is socially unacceptable to say that? Here again we can ask: Is this statement based upon objective investigation of what native speakers do and do not find acceptable in a particular situation, or does it merely represent the private judgement of the teacher or linguist, or the prejudices of his social group or class?"

The verbal assignments must always be corrected in terms of pronunciation, presentation, stress, posture, delivery, and a number of other things. Written assignments are always corrected through spelling, grammar, punctuation, tense and agreement. Then there are listening assignments and all have to be corrected.

It is in this concept of correction that the whole program takes misleading proportions. It misleads students to believe that they have an erroneous existence outside of the classroom. Thanks to Pit Corder we now realize that these corrections are not based on objectivity but on subjective intuitive, private (and sometimes biased) knowledge.

When this uncertainty is gilded with an appearance of unquestionable knowledge, this misleading pedagogy takes the proportion of an oppressive structure.

Language teaching is also an oppressive pedagogy in many other forms. It changes the transforming and liberating power of the word into idle chatter and verbalism. The same word that is so important, so relevant, so full of meaning and life, so pertinent to the existence of that child, is denied its meaning in the classroom setting. The child perceives its existence in silence or is nourished by false words that have lost their potency. Freire explains the liberating force of the word: "But while to say the true word—which is work, which is praxis—is to transform the world, saying the word is not the privilege of some few men, but the right of every man. Consequently, no one cay say a true word alone— nor can he say it for another, in a prescriptive act which robs others of their words."[4] This denial of the word is an act of aggression which makes language teaching painfully oppressive.

Paulo Freire discusses the ways in which teaching reflects an oppressive society and this is so very true, especially for language teaching:

(a) The teacher teaches, and the students are taught.
(b) The teacher knows everything, and the students know nothing.
(c) The teacher thinks, and the students are thought about.
(d) The teacher talks and the students listen-meekly.
(e) The teacher disciplines and the students are disciplined.
(f) The teacher chooses and enforces his choice, and the students comply.
(g) The teacher acts and the students have the illusion of acting through the action of the teacher.
(h) The teacher chooses the program content, and the students (who were not consulted) adapt to it.
(i) The teacher confuses the authority of knowledge with his own professional authority, which he sets in opposition to the freedom of the students.

(j) The teacher is the subject of the learning process, while the pupils are mere objects.[5]

It is clear from Freire's implications that the student has lost his critical consciousness and his existence now becomes a dependency. He is oppressed to the extent that he cannot think, or act, or respond without the corrective values of the teacher and this has created so much confusion.

Any rebellion against this status quo, oppressive though it is, leaves the student alienated and marginated. Since the teacher wields the power over the psychic consciousness of the other students, it becomes very simple to ostracize one student based solely on the will of the teacher. This creates fear in the student, and fear is the root of linguistic impotence.

Implicit in this teacher-knows-it-all policy is the assumption that the student exists only in the world of the teacher, not with the real world or with others; that the student is a spectator, not a recreator. Generally the knowledge of the teacher, as far as the world is concerned, is very limited. It is mostly the student and hardly the teacher that beats with pulse of society and is more acquainted with the new linguistic terms generated by the society.

Generally, most of these terms are themselves an act of rebellion against the oppressive linguistic classroom pedagogy. The students are tired of being told what to say and what not to say, how to say it and how not to say it, and so many dos and don'ts that they generate their own linguistic structures. This creation is liberating, firstly, because it protects the student from the world of the teacher who is unable to understand the student and can only revert to the old cliché that it is bad language. Secondly, and more importantly, however, is that the student has generated a new perception of human existence and has discovered the liberating word that sets him free from the oppressive classroom pedagogy. The subtlest form of control and manipulation of man by man is the guise of language teaching in the classroom.

NOTES

1. Paulo Freire, *Pedagogy of the Oppressed* (New York: Seabury Press, 1970), 57.
2. Pit Corder, *Introducing Applied Linguistics* (Middlesex, England: Penguin Books, 1973), 19.
3. Ibid., 19.
4. Freire, *Pedagogy of the Oppressed*, 76.
5. Ibid., 59.

Twelve

Leave Language Alone

If it's working don't try to fix it.

The growth of language, like the growth of civilization, is not deliberate but evolutionary. Those who try to speed up the evolutionary process by artificial catalysts may very well find that the catalysis ends in dissolution and decay. Forced development is synonymous with negative development and resembles the language of the colonizers who forced their development on an unsuspecting people. It is the paradox of Kurtz in Conrad's *Heart of Darkness*, who is the ideal of a successful colonizer and yet the embodiment of human degradation and deterioration.

The quest for linguistic domination carries with it the superimposition of a whole cultural aura, and the conquered are treated no better than wild beasts that need to be trained. They are referred to as uncultured, and the conquerors adopt the strange notion that they have to teach these primitive people how to speak. No one stops to think that these supposedly subculture people have had a language of their own for as long as they existed, and this language has worked well to serve their needs and is more suited for the landscape and culture of their existence. How can we reasonably expect that these people are to be "taught" language?

All languages of every dialectal variation have been learned rather than taught. The teaching of any language that has its use outside of the societal arena of human interaction makes that language stilted, irrelevant, and absurd. Even the most sophisticated teacher has to learn before he teaches, and the fallacy that a university degree in English prepares one for teaching English is evident. Since language grows in the interaction of individuals within a speech community, then we must look for the lines of demarcation that set the boundaries of a specific language within that speech community. It is within this community that we must discover the linguistic variations—the phonemic and phonetic differences, its lexical choices and changes, its syntactic acceptance and rejection.

Over the years man has succeeded to a great extent in destroying nature's resources under the guise of development. Some societies do the same in the psychological realm, where nature's gift of speech is concerned. Maybe man has become so degenerate that it becomes difficult to distinguish between man's achievement and nature's gift.

If we perceive the acquisition of language as an achievement of our own genius—the genius of being able to teach a little child to speak—then, indeed, we can manipulate the educatee's existence. Then we will be taking the omniscient role of absolute teaching, and this in itself is a philosophy of nonliberation.

If, however, we perceive linguistic ability as one of nature's greatest gifts to man, then surely, we will show some respect for everyone's language and everyone's dialect, because we will then begin to believe that nature has been kind to us all without discrimination. Man's linguistic competence is the same universally and his development in society has been nurtured by the society in which he grows. Nature makes no linguistic distinction between the rich and the poor or between geographical locations. It is we, with our concepts of development, our inherent discrimination and prejudice, and our selfish desires to manipulate the lives of other people, that assign linguistic abilities into prejudicial categories. We refuse the other person as an equal and so one of the ways of asserting our superiority is by negating him of his language and having him learn to speak like us. All it needs for one to adopt the role of the domesticator is to have more power. Domination can evolve through fire power, political power, economic power or social power.

The language-learning program, therefore, is the simple show of who wields more power in a specific community. It is no better than political dictators and fascism or economic monopoly of multinational corporations. Whereas nuclear warfare by the superpowers threatens the physical life of people, the subtler control by the super linguistic world destroys the psyche of millions and negates the very existence of people.

The United Nations Charter of Human Rights gives much credence to the fact that all men are equal. It is a task of all linguists, language teachers, school administrators, and anyone who has anything to do with language interaction among people to recognize the following basic linguistic rights:

1. That all languages, irrespective of the social, economic or cultural context are equal and each language has the potential to be creative, innovative, and to mean what the speaker intends it to mean.

2. That linguistically all human beings are born with the same potential for language use and that language competence does not differ based on colour, class, creed, or any other external force. Therefore, given a specific speech community, any person can learn the language of that speech community provided that he/she is initiated into that community during the formative years.

3. That a language of human being embodies the whole cultural and psychological existence of that person and that the individual has had no control over the language acquired.

Therefore, the denial of that native language is a denial of that person's very existence and consequently is one of the most dehumanizing experiences a person can have.

Based on the above, every single dialect in every existing speech community should be given credence by all other speech communities, and especially by linguists and educators.

Thirteen

Get Rid of Schooled-up Language

School is a bad place for kids.

The concept of delanguage teaching presupposes the basic linguistic rights of every human being. The problems associated with the language education program have been the perpetual bane in the lives of all concerned with language teaching. Every year we hear of better methods, new innovations, modern examinations, revised texts, and before long, our golden dreams are changed to nightmares and we have committed ourselves to a diligent exercise in futility. Considering all the damage that the language instruction program has done to innocent children around the world the solution seems nothing less than delanguage teaching.

Basically, all communities should begin to regard literacy as a norm. From childhood we need to develop the habit of being literate. Most people who are literate will confess that they have acquired literacy not from school but from some social pressure or some program within the family or societal structure.

The two basic facets of language learning are listening and speaking, and it is impossible for one hour a day, five days a week classroom activities to teach these basic skills which are in use every waking moment of an individual's life. Teaching is done by precept and by example, and the classroom contradiction is that the teacher wants to teach listening skills, but he himself is not prepared to listen to the language or the students.

Listening skills are learned from birth. In the process of a child's acquisition of language there is a 'silent period,' during which the child listens and makes association between meaning and sound. The first process of learning language is the process of listening. The so-called primitive people have a much more profound language because they have taken time to listen to the language of nature—the voice of the waterfall and the whispering of the breeze—they speak and we listen so that we can also speak.

All members of a speech community should be encouraged to listen to other people speaking, and whereas they must appreciate the language spoken by everyone, they will at the same time listen to the context of each mode of communication. The situational approach is, therefore, inherent in the life of the individual and he learns language by living language. Radio, television, and other audio-visual equipment can also serve as a secondary program to develop listening skills.

At birth, the child has the innate ability to utter every linguistic sound from all human languages. This child has the ability to speak and society determines what language he will speak. As he grows up, he is sent to school to learn an unfamiliar code of communication that is only rarely used in the world of his existence. The better way is from very early in life (during the formative years) the child should be exposed to the whole continuum of linguistic-societal patterns. Because of the ability to deal with language acquisition at that age, the child's ability will supersede the bidialectal phenomenon and will develop what can more aptly be described as a multidialectal competence.

Speech, therefore, becomes less of a tedious effort to conform to someone else's idiolect and it becomes a more natural and comfortable program. The spoken language taught in the classroom breathes an air of artificiality and robs verbal communication of its naturalness. The spoken word cannot be contained within walls, but it must be made flesh to dwell among people.

Speech is learned by the positive and negative reinforcement of the community, and the singularity of a teacher's pedagogy can never capture the world of spoken communication. Speech is best learned and best used in the community and not the classroom.

Reading and writing are secondary linguistic functions and, as such, come after listening and speech. It is fallacious to assume that because a language is not written or read that it is inferior. Writing and reading have to do with necessity and classroom boredom is fostered when teachers present a reading passage based on what goes on the other side of the world.

Literacy programs have to do with interest and people will tend to read what they are interested in. The same holds true for writing and students show a far greater proficiency if they write something they are interested in. In an experiment in Freeport (see appendix 6) it is shown that learning to read and write becomes enjoyable and easy if interest is maintained. Literacy, therefore, can easily be the responsibility of the community and of the media, and even of the home.

Maybe other than having formal classroom teaching it would be more beneficial if the so-called experts concentrate more on descriptive linguistics. If we have a board of descriptive linguists who would daily or weekly publish for the benefit of the community, changes in speech patterns and trends in usage, then members of the speech community can refer to that group at any time or can challenge the group or any of its propositions.

Through participation, therefore, everyone becomes involved in learning and teaching language, and the board of descriptive linguists must not exist as an omniscient body but must realize that the community has designated a role to which they are asked to dedicate their time and effort. The board is not there because they know more than others, but the board exists because everyone cannot spend time with the same activity.

Fourteen

Language as Arts and Science

The whole is greater than the sum of its parts.
—Lionel Trilling

The study of language can be examined at two levels: (a) language as a science and (b) language as an art. Each in itself faces severe restrictions, because language has to do with life, and it is not a paradox to say in this case that the whole is greater than the sum of its parts. Nevertheless, for the sake of analysis we shall tolerate this seeming bisection.

LANGUAGE AS A SCIENCE

Indeed it is interesting to know about the language that one speaks. It is a formidable experience (if you are interested) in knowing the Latin roots of words and the Greek words that were engrafted to the English language. But imagine having to study Chaucer without having to consider the content of his poetry. Certainly that is sublime insanity. So the scientific study of language must have both purpose and perspective. Whereas, it is an advantage to know about the language, it does not necessarily follow that if you know about the language, you know the language. This has been a significant confusion in the same way that people confuse knowing about God with knowing God. Maybe the whole programme of identifying parts of speech, person, number, case, tense, et cetera, is all an exercise in futility if the original intention is to develop language proficiency.

Yet man has never been satisfied with an abstract acceptance of realities. It is not enough that the sun comes up in the morning and goes down in the evening. The how, when, why, and where- fore of every detail must be worked out, and men are prepared to give their lives for seemingly new truths. This quest for the definitive also holds true for the world of linguistics. It is, therefore, acceptable that people should devote time to the study of linguistics. Certainly people will like to know the phonemes of a language, the phonetic variations, the syntactic structures, and the possible transformations. It is an excellent idea to be able to categorize nouns in terms of proper, common, collective, and abstract. The study of deep structures and surface structures can be very revealing, and to enquire into the ways the brain controls language is a fascinating experience.

The fallacy exists in the assumption that the study of any one of these things will make you a better language user. The scientific study of language can be regarded as a quest to concretise a part of the abstract in the same way that man examines a rock from the moon to determine how the universe was created. This kind of study is permitted for the few who are interested, but cannot and must not be pushed upon all members of the community.

Delanguage teaching erases the forcible learning of irrelevant linguistic rules. The rules that are important would be internalized by the student anyhow in the same way that a normal two-year-old child would have internalized hundreds of linguistic rules that an adult who is learning a second language takes years to internalize.

LANGUAGE AS AN ART

The use of new jargons in the language-teaching program is indicative of new approaches. Educators and linguists seem to want to introduce language-arts programs in terms of *Use of English, Language for Living, and English for Life.** All these seem to suggest that the main thrust is the art of using language in one's everyday existence.

The use of language as an art has to do with the context, the intention, the intonation, and hundreds of variables. The three simple words, "I love you," can mean dozens of things to dozens of people. The art of language usage is to fulfill, in behavioral terms the objective that one has set out to achieve. The parent who tells his children, "I love you," must eventually achieve the aim of making the children believe that they are loved by him and must even reciprocate, where appropriate, this love.

The boy who brings a bunch of roses on Valentine's Day and presents it to the girl in the next office with the words, "I love you," is probably looking for something more lasting and more permanent. But there are so many other things associated with the context that it is impossible to identify every linguistic variation and place them in every single context. This double impossibility occurs because first, a context is never exhaustive or static; in fact it is very dynamic, and we can encounter situations that we did not think would possibly exist. Second, we can never exhaust the possible number of linguistic combinations, because language is innovative, creative and adaptable, and even unheard combinations like "moon-set" conjure some degree of meaning in our minds. Lewis Carroll's nonsense rhyme, "Twas Brillig and the slithy toves . . . " is not really nonsense but has in it some profound depth of meaning.

Language as an art can never be taught in the classroom because the classroom limits itself to textbooks that are outdated before they printed and the classroom does not provide real-life situations. In fact, the classroom-oriented language programme is a further process in alienation.

*Titles of English textbooks used in schools.

Fifteen

Free, Free at Last

I must be free to think, to shape my world.

That which underlies all language experience, is that language is not taught, it is learned. It is not a package handed over to someone, or a formula that can be passed on from one person to another. This concept that someone can learn to speak properly is an experience that cannot be taught or handed down—it can only be experienced.

The only possible way that one may attempt to enhance the richness of creativity in language is by a process of human interaction. This interaction can never be on the basis of a teacher-student, or educator-educatee relationship. Once the individual has passed the stage of acquiring the functional use of language in his society, copying modes of communication becomes humiliating and erratic. The interaction of equality is inconceivable in the language instruction program of the classroom. This is why students find it far more tolerable and enjoyable to interact linguistically with their peers. Their creativity is at its best and expression knows not the limits of formalism and uncreative exactitude. Only the voice, the intonation, the body language, and the involvement of the listeners matter. In this setting, communication does take place, and it is a communication of nonrestraint, emitting the very personality and emotion of the speaker.

By contrast the teacher-student interaction destroys the intuitive and imaginative self of the student and his language loses power and potency. Galileo said that "Teaching is an act of love." It would be equally accurate, and maybe more revealing to juxtapose that language development is an act of love. Language instruction without equality and without love is nothing better than language destruction.

Paulo Freire infers this linguistic interaction in terms of dialogue. He makes the following profound statements:

> Dialogue is the encounter between men, mediated by the world, in order to name the world. Hence, dialogue cannot occur between those who want to name the world and those whose right to speak has been denied them. . .
>
> If it is in speaking their word that men, by naming the world, transform it, dialogue imposes itself as the way by which men achieve significance as men. Dialogue is thus an existential necessity. And since dialogue is the encounter in which the united reflection and action of the dialoguers are addressed to the humanized, this dialogue cannot be reduced to the act of one person's "depositing" ideas in another, nor can it become a simple exchange of ideas to be "consumed by the discussants". .
>
> Dialogue cannot exist, however, in the absence of a profound love for the world and for men. The naming of the world in an act of creation and re-creation, is not possible if it is not infused with love. Love is at the same time the foundation of dialogue and dialogue itself. It is thus necessarily the task of responsible subjects and cannot exist in a relation of domination. . . .
>
> On the other hand, dialogue cannot exist without humility. The naming of the world, through which men constantly recreate that world, cannot be an act of arrogance. Dialogue, as the encounter of men addressed to the common task of learning and acting, is broken if the parties [or one of them] lack humility. How can I dialogue if I always project ignorance onto others and never perceive my own. . . . .
>
> Dialogue further requires an intense faith in man, faith in his vocation to be more fully human [which is not the privilege of an elite, but the birthright of all men]. Faith in man is an "a priori" requirement for dialogue; the "dialogical man" believes in other men even before he meets them face to face. . . .

Founding itself upon love, humility, and faith, dialogue becomes a horizontal relationship of which mutual trust between the dialoguers is the logical consequence....[1]

This kind of linguistic liberation can be a very shattering experience for those who have used language to maintain psychological superiority. For many it represents a destruction of years of quest to speak like someone else. But this shattering can also be a very liberating experience.

It is liberating first because it leads to the discovery of the self, and that self is no longer the self of arrogance, but becomes a very human self. In that discovery of the self is a discovery of the world through the living word, and an enjoyment of the world through the relatedness of this word. But it is not only appreciation and discovery of the world, it is a constant creation and recreation, a shaping and reshaping that synthesize in a strange mutation; but a mutation that is very powerful, very creative, and very free. In this combination lies the discovery of a higher existence, through the mediator of the liberating word.

Second, it is liberating because one is now free to think and to act in a way that is not constrained by self-importance, arrogance, or prejudice. The language that shapes our thought becomes a tool to be used for creating structures of love, joy, and peace. Language ceases to become a master to manipulate us and to condition the trend of our thought. Liberating language has the experience of one who has emerged from a dark prison.

Third, liberating linguistics is pertinent because the object of domination is now relieved of the burden of inferiority complex. There will no longer be the struggle to become someone else whose ideal we can never attain. The struggle to exist in an uncreatable world will come to an end, and the force of the creative word will crystalize structures of human interaction and of true humanity. The oppressed will no longer live in a marginated world, but by his ability to communicate and to create will contribute to a very meaningful life.

All the above hold true for the classroom context, where the student represents the oppressed and the teacher, the oppressor. Delanguage teaching would eliminate even the concept of this interaction and linguistic participation will become a mutually intelligible and intelligent bipartisan process.

Maybe on that day, students and teachers alike will put aside all misunderstandings and futility of the language-teaching program, and will join hand in hand to sing "Free at last, free at last. Thank God Almighty I'm free at last."

NOTES

1. Paulo Freire, *Pedagogy of the Oppressed* (New York: Seabury Press, 1970), 76-80.

APPENDICES

Appendix I

BAHAMIAN EXAMS

Bahamas Junior Certificate Examination written at grade nine level. Students must pass at least five subjects with English and Math before they are promoted to grade ten.

BRITISH EXAMS

1. General Certificate of Education Examination-ordinary and advanced levels—administered by University of London (grades eleven to thirteen)
2. Pitman's Exams
3. Royal Society of Arts Exams

NORTH AMERICAN EXAMS

1. S.A.T.
2. P.S.A.T.

Appendix II

Most linguists represent the Creole continuum thus:

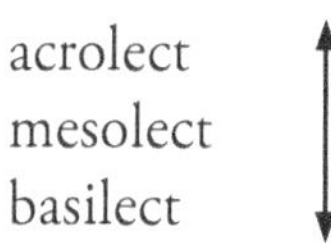

Others, in an effort to show less partiality, represent it as:

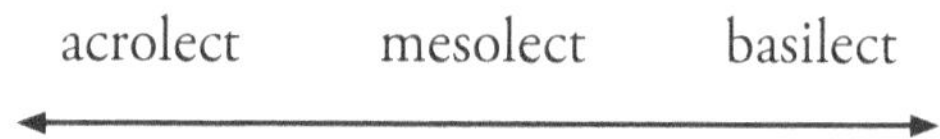

There is still a covert preference for acrolect in the second diagram.

Appendix III

SAINT PAUL'S COLLEGE GRADES 11-12
1983 AND 1984

Two students in two consecutive years were taken out of the Non G.C.E. group (set 2) and put into G.C.E. group (set 1). Positive reinforcement was given throughout the year, and in both instances the students were successful at the G.C.E. exams.

In another instance, student X was made to believe that she was an A student in English and this was reinforced in the classroom. When the student took the G.C.E. exams, student X had an A. The following year, this reinforcement was omitted and student X was made to believe that she was not that good after all. When she took an examination of equal difficulty to the G.C.E., she failed. Other students in the same class who previously failed the G.C.E. were given positive reinforcement and they passed the exam.

Appendix IV

Saint Paul's College, like most high schools in the Bahamas, divides a grade of English students into sets:

1. Set One is generally the best set with more brilliant students. These are the students who are preordained to do the external examinations.
2. Set Two consists of average students who will do some of the examinations (e.g., Pitman) but will not be allowed to do G.C.E.'s.
3. Set Three in practice is labeled "dumb," and students are expected to perform that way.

The grades of these sets are "fixed" so that a person in set I will get A—C; set II will get C—D; and set III will get D—E.

Appendix V

A group of students from Saint Paul's College has been working on a research project on Bahamian folklore and Bahamian dialect. Several field trips have been made and it is anticipated that this project will be published shortly.

Appendix VI

Literacy teaching to adult students was done in Freeport. In one specific instance, the student was a mason and found it much more comfortable to read the instructions on cement sacks. His written assignments also reflect his professional preference.

Bibliography

Bennett, W. A. *Aspects of Language and Language Teaching.* London: Cambridge University Press, 1968.

Bernstein, Basil. *Class, Codes, and Control: Theoretical Studies toward a Sociology of Language*, vol. 1. London: Routledge and Kegan Paul, 1973.

Best, John W. *Research in Education.* Englewood Cliffs, New Jersey: Prentice Hall, Inc., 1970.

Brazil, David. *The True Book about Our Language.* London: Frederick Miller, 1965.

Britton, James. "English Teaching: Retrospect and Prospect." *English in Education* 15, no. 2 (Summer 1981), 1.

Carroll, Lewis. *Alice in Wonderland.* Middlesex, England: Penguin Books, 1962.

Caute, David. Fanon. London: Wm. Collins and Company, 1970.

Cave, George. *Some Problems of Language in Guyana.* Turkeyen: University of Guyana, 1972.

Cave, Ronald. *An Introduction to Curriculum Development.* London: Warlock Educational, 1971.

Chomsky, Noam. *Children with Learning Problems.* Edited by Edward Sapir et al. New York: Brunner/Nazel, 1973.

Corder, Pit S. *Introducing Applied Linguistics.* Middlesex, England: Penguin Books, 1973.

Craig, Dennis. *Pidginization and Creolization of Languages.* London: Cambridge University Press, 1971.

Dawson, Helaine S. *On the Outskirts of Hope*-Educating Youth from Poverty Areas. New York: McGraw-Hill, 1968.

Douglas, Keens Paul. "Communication and the Arts." *Caribbean Con- fact* (October 1984), 11.

Decamp, David. *Pidginization and Creolization of Languages.* Edited by Dell Hymes. London: Cambridge University Press, 1971.

Edwards, V. K. "The West Indian Language Issue in British Schools." *Language in Society* 9, no. 3 (December 1980)

Fannon, Frantz. *The Wretched of the Earth*. New York: Grove Press, 1968.

Freire, Paulo. *Pedagogy of the Oppressed*. New York: Seabury Press, 1988.

French, F. G. *The Teaching of English Abroad,* parts I, II, and III. London: Oxford University Press, 1950.

Finich, Curtis, et al. *Curriculum Development in Vocational and Technical Education*. Boston: Allyn and Bacon, 1979.

Hymes, Dell, ed. *Pidginization and Creolization of Language*. London: Cambridge University Press, 1971.

Illich, Ivan. *Deschooling Society*. New York: Harper and Row, 1983.

Kerr, John. *Changing the Curriculum*. London: University at London Press, 1970.

Lefevre, Carl and Helen. *Writing by Patterns*. New York: Alfred A. Knopf, 1978.

McLeod, A. "Writing Dialect and Linguistic Awareness." *English in Education* 15, no. 2 (Summer 1981), 26.

Mager, Robert F. *Preparing Instructional Objectives*. California: Pitman Learning, 1975.

Martin, Rachel. "A Conversation with Ira Shor." *Literary Research Center* 2, no. 1 (Spring 1986), 26.

Nash, Roy. *Schooling in Rural Societies*. London: Methuen and Co., 1980.

Ponge, Robert. "Foreign Language Teaching and the Two Cultures." *Savocou*, September 1975.

Ramphal, Dwarka. "The Teaching of Tense and Agreements in Fourth Forms at Covent Garden Secondary School. The Creolese Parallel Approach." Thesis, University of Guyana, 1971.

Ramphal, Kennard. "An Analysis of Reading Instruction Offered to West Indian Creole-Speaking Students." Ph.D. dissertation, University of Toronto, 1983.

Robinatt, Betty Wallace. *Teaching English to Speakers of Other Languages*. Minneapolis: University of Minnesota Press, 1980.

Shilling, Alison, and John Holm. *Dictionary of Bahamian English*. New York: Lexik House, 1982.

Shuy, Roger, ed. *Linguistic Theory: What Can It Say about Reading?* Newark: International Reading Association, 1977.

Sledd, James. "Bidialectalism: The Linguistics of White Supremancy," *English Journal* 58, no. 9 (1969), 1307-29.

Tashlik, Phyllis, "Introducing Reader's Theater," *Journal of Reading* 22, no. 3 (December 1978), 216.

Trent, J. D., J. S. Trent and D. J. O'Neill. *Concepts in Communication.* Boston: Allyn and Bacon, Inc., 1973.

Tyler, Ralph. *Basic Principles of Curriculum and Instruction.* Chicago: University of Chicago Press, 1949.

Vigdor, Suzanne, "The Speech Teacher is the Reading Teacher's Friend," *Reading Teacher* 31 No. 6 (March 1978), 612.

Vygotsky, L. S. *Thought and Language.* Boston: Massachusetts Institute of Technology, 1962.

www.ingramcontent.com/pod-product-compliance
Lightning Source LLC
Chambersburg PA
CBHW020121310726
48970CB00002B/729